FORCES

BY
JOANNA BRUNDLE

KU-442-580

SCIENCE IN ACTION

©2018
Book Life
King's Lynn
Norfolk PE30 4LS

ISBN: 978-1-78637-225-3

All rights reserved
Printed in Malaysia

A catalogue record for this book
is available from the British Library.

Written by:
Joanna Brundle

Edited by:
Kirsty Holmes

Designed by:
Drue Rintoul

Photocredits
Abbreviations: l-left, r-right, b-bottom, t-top, c-centre, m-middle.

Front Cover t – pedrosala. Front Cover mt – MrSegui. Front Cover mb – SIHASAKPRACHUM. Front Cover b – 3Dsculptor. 1 – cristiano barni. 2 – MarchCattle. 4t – Africa Studio. 4b – Daniel M. Nagy. 5t – Castleski. 5b – michaelstephan-fotografie. 6tr – MidoSemsem. 6l – Nicku. 6br – kirilldz. 7tr – Nicku. 7l – Jorg Hackemann. 7b – wavebreakmedia. 8t – Jacob Lund. 8b – TijanaM. 9t – Brian Kinney. 9b – Bartosz Nitkiewicz. 10 – Soloviova Liudmyla. 11tr – Pavel L Photo and Video. 11tl – Africa Studio. 11b – Kaspars Grinvalds. 12tr – wavebreakmedia. 12l – Olimpik. 12b – Danny Smythe, Elizabeth Chapman. 13t – Vadim Sadovski. 13b – Khoroshunova Olga. 14tr – desertfox99. 14l – Africa Studio. 14b – imagedb.com. 15t – udaix. 15b – Triff. 16tr – Ralf Maassen (DTEurope). 16bm – sit. 16b – Stacey Lynn Payne. 17t – SamL. 17bm – ktsdesign. 17b – freevideophotoagency. 18bl – thieury. 18br – My Good Images. 19tr – vincent noel. 19mr – tanuha2001. 19b – Mtsaride. 20t – Krivosheev Vitaly. 20b – wavebreakmedia. 21tr – claudio zaccherini. 21b – Sheila Fitzgerald. 22 – Ilike. 23t – Mari Swanepoel. 23b – Pixachi. 24tr – Asia Images Group. 24b – JIANG HONGYAN. 25t – Jakub Janele. 25r, 25b – donatas1205. 26tr – frantic00. 26bl – szefei. 26br – Andrey_Popov. 27tl – StockPhotosArt. 27tr – Dja65. 27ml – ILYA AKINSHIN. 27mr – Ansis Klucis. 27b – Yodsapat Puasupacharoen. 28tr – Taweesak Jaroensin. 28bl – Wallenrock. 28br – Bplanet. 29t – Colin Porteous. 29b – Michael Stokes. 30t – ntstudio. 30m – Kyselova Inna, Seregam. 30b – koosen.
Images are courtesy of Shutterstock.com. With thanks to Getty Images, Thinkstock Photo and iStockphoto.

CONTENTS

Words that look like **this** are explained in the glossary on page 31.

WHAT ARE FORCES?

You may have heard people talk about 'forces that govern the universe', but what are forces and how do they affect our lives?

PUSHES AND PULLS

Forces push and pull on objects. They cause objects to start or stop moving, to change direction or shape, and to **attract** or **repel** other objects.

Forces are not **physical** things that we can see and touch, like a desk or a pen. But although forces are invisible, we can feel and see their effects all around us. Think about a book, sitting on the table in front of you. You can pull it towards you or push it away. The book is being pulled towards the ground by **gravity**, which stops it from floating around the room. The table resists – or acts against – this pulling force. If you push the book off the table, the table can no longer resist the pull of gravity and the book falls to the ground. As you read, you use pulling forces to turn the pages and pushing forces to close the book.

Squashing the lemon **exerts** a force on it that changes its shape.

The sledge is moving because it is being pushed and pulled in the same direction.

Mass is not a force. The mass of an object is how much **matter** it contains. An object's mass is usually measured in grams or kilograms. Weight, on the other hand, is a force. The weight of an object is worked out by combining its mass with the downward force of gravity. Scientists measure weight in **newtons** (N), but in everyday life, weight is usually measured in grams and kilograms.

The mass of an astronaut is the same on Earth and on the Moon. However, the force of gravity is much stronger on Earth than it is on the Moon. This means that objects weigh around six times more on Earth than they do on the Moon. Because of this, an astronaut on the Moon would find it easy to pick up a large rock that would be too heavy to carry on Earth.

This astronaut, from the U.S.A., is standing on the Moon.

MARKING FORCES

Forces are marked on diagrams and pictures by arrows. The direction of the arrow shows the direction the force is acting in. The bigger the arrow is, the greater the force.

Pulling Forces

Downwards Pushing Force

Downwards Pushing Force

In this game of tug-of-war, both dogs are pulling equally, so the arrow is the same size in both directions. Both dogs are also exerting a downwards force on the ground.

5

FORCES AND MOTION

PAST DISCOVERIES

In the fourth century **B.C.**, the ancient Greek **philosopher**, Aristotle, tried to explain how forces make things move.

Aristotle thought that a moving object must have a force pushing on it at all times to keep it moving. He was wrong! His idea did not explain, for example, why an arrow keeps moving through the air even after it has left the bow.

Aristotle

Galileo Galilei

Galileo's **theory** of inertia explains why an arrow keeps moving until air resistance (see page 16) or the pushing force of a target stops it.

In the late 1500's, the Italian scientist Galileo Galilei realised that when he rolled a ball along a flat surface, it kept going without any force pushing or pulling it. He had discovered inertia – the fact that things that are moving will keep moving, and things that are still will keep still. He worked out that the ball didn't start moving until he pushed it and it only stopped moving when another force acted on it. Inertia itself is not a force.

ISAAC NEWTON

In the same year that Galileo died, 1642, a brilliant English scientist called Isaac Newton was born. Newton described how forces make things move. He called his ideas the three Laws of Motion. His first law builds on Galileo's ideas about inertia. It states that a moving object that isn't being pushed or pulled by any force must keep moving in a straight line and at a constant speed. The object will only change speed or direction if a force pushes or pulls on it.

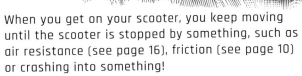
When you get on your scooter, you keep moving until the scooter is stopped by something, such as air resistance (see page 16), friction (see page 10) or crashing into something!

Newton's Second Law of Motion is about acceleration. Acceleration is how quickly something speeds up when it is moving. You can feel acceleration when you're in a car that quickly moves away from traffic lights. Newton worked out that many forces make objects accelerate. The lighter the object is and the greater the force being exerted on it, the faster the acceleration will be.

If you push the pedals on your bike faster, you will move forwards faster. Racing bikes are made of very light materials to help riders accelerate quickly.

7

Newton worked out that forces – which he called actions – happen in pairs. When there is a force pushing in one direction, there will always be another force pushing in the opposite direction. Newton's third law states that every action has an equal and opposite reaction. When a fish swims, for example, it pushes water backwards using its fins. The water then pushes the fish forwards with the same force.

If you push off from the side of a swimming pool by pushing your feet against the wall, you exert a force on the wall. At the same time, the wall resists the force and pushes back in the opposite direction. This has the effect of pushing you forwards. The harder you push, the faster you move away from the wall and through the water.

When you jump over a skipping rope, your feet exert a pushing force on the ground. The ground pushes back with equal force in the opposite direction. Although the forces are equal, the effects are not! Although you can't see it, the Earth actually moves downwards when you jump upwards – but, while you jump high into the air, the Earth barely moves at all.

CAN YOU FEEL THE FORCE?

Just as the acceleration of a fast car can push you back into your seat, slowing down can make you feel like you're being pushed forwards. Slowing down is called deceleration. You feel pushed sideways when you go round a corner very quickly. All this pushing that you feel isn't really a force – it's inertia trying to keep you travelling in a straight line at a steady speed. The feeling of getting pushed around by inertia is called g-force.

When a rollercoaster changes speed and direction, different g-forces act on the body. At the top of a slope, you feel weightless and you may even lift off the seat! At the bottom of the slope, a g-force of three makes your body feel three times heavier than normal. Pilots of fighter aeroplanes are trained to deal with g-forces up to nine g. G-forces this high push the blood out of the pilot's head and into his or her legs. This would cause someone without special training or equipment to pass out.

NORMAL GRAVITY HAS A G-FORCE OF ONE. THERE IS ONE G OF FORCE ACTING ON YOU AS YOU READ THIS BOOK.

FRICTION

Friction is a slowing force that happens when two surfaces rub against each other. Even surfaces that look really smooth are actually covered in tiny bumps and dips. When two surfaces rub together, the bumps and dips catch on one another and slow the objects down. Whenever anything moves or tries to move, friction occurs. Friction will eventually cause moving objects to stop. It is also the force that stops still objects from beginning to move. If friction acts only on one side of a moving object, it can change the direction of the object by making it spin. This is what happens when a skateboarder presses down on one end of the board to make it turn sharply.

STATIC AND SLIDING FRICTION

There are two kinds of friction: static friction and sliding friction. Static friction is much stronger and makes it difficult to move an object that is still.

LOOK AT THE PATTERNS ON YOUR FINGERTIPS. THE TINY RIDGES OF SKIN THAT MAKE UP FINGERPRINTS ARE ACTUALLY THERE TO PROVIDE FRICTION. THEY HELP US TO PICK THINGS UP AND HOLD ON TO THEM.

Static friction makes a heavy shopping trolley hard to move! Once the trolley is moving, it's much easier to push. At that stage, only sliding friction is trying to stop it moving.

10

Friction gives us **grip** and stops objects from sliding away. Without friction, we wouldn't be able to walk, ride a bicycle or drive a car. Rough surfaces increase the amount of friction that is produced. This is why it's harder to push your finger over a piece of sandpaper than it is to push it over a page of this book.

The rough pattern - or 'tread' - on these tyres helps the truck to grip in slippery conditions.

Friction is increased if two surfaces are pressed together. When you apply the brakes on your bicycle, the friction caused by the brake pads pressing on the wheel slows you down.

Smooth surfaces reduce friction. Ice skaters glide easily over the ice because there is very little friction between the thin, smooth blades of the skates and the smooth ice.

Lubricants are slippery liquids that reduce friction by helping surfaces to slide past one another easily. Oil is a lubricant that is used to coat the moving parts of machines, such as the parts in car engines. Oil stops the parts from damaging and wearing one another away. Some solids can act as lubricants too. Graphite, a form of carbon, is a solid lubricant found in the lead of pencils. It makes a pencil easy to write with because it slips easily from the pencil point onto paper, leaving a black line.

Smooth metal balls, called **bearings**, in the wheels of roller blades and skateboards reduce friction and help the wheels to turn freely.

11

GRAVITY

When you hear the word 'gravity', you probably think about the pulling force that the Earth exerts on us and everything around us.

In fact, all objects that have mass exert this pulling force on one another. The strength of gravity's pulling force depends on the mass of the objects and the distance between them. Objects are attracted to the Earth because it has a large mass and so exerts a strong pull. The further away objects are from the Earth, the less the Earth's gravity can be felt. In space, astronauts become weightless. Their distance from the Earth means that the pull of Earth's gravity can no longer be felt.

It's hard work climbing stairs because we feel the effect of gravity trying to pull us down.

Gravity tries to pull objects to the centre of the Earth – that's why things fall down holes!

Isaac Newton was the first person to explain how gravity works. He watched an apple fall from a tree and worked out that the force pulling on the apple must be the same as the force that pulls on the Moon and planets.

DID YOU KNOW? SCIENTISTS REFER TO GRAVITY AS THE FORCE OF ATTRACTION.

GRAVITY AND SPACE

Billions of years ago, the force of gravity pulled swirling dust and gas clouds together to form planets and stars. The Sun sits at the centre of the solar system and its gravitational pull extends trillions of kilometres into space. The Earth **orbits** the Sun because the Sun's force of gravity is much stronger than Earth's. In fact, it is 27 times stronger! So how do planets manage to stay in orbit? Why doesn't the Earth crash into the Sun? It's because planets have a forward movement, which balances the force of gravity from the planet that they are orbiting.

Jupiter is the largest planet in the solar system and has many moons. They orbit Jupiter because of its powerful gravitational pull.

TIDES

Every day, the oceans on Earth rise and fall. These changes are called the tides. They are caused by the Moon's gravity, which literally lifts the water on Earth to create a tidal bulge. On the other side of the Earth, the Moon's pull causes a slight movement of the Earth towards the Moon. Water rushes in to fill the gap, causing a high tide there too. As the Earth spins, different parts of its surface are affected.

DID YOU KNOW?
TIDES EXIST IN LAKES AND RIVERS TOO, EVEN IN YOUR BATH WATER! HOWEVER, THE MASS OF THESE BODIES OF WATER IS TINY COMPARED WITH THAT OF AN OCEAN. THIS MEANS THAT THE PULL OF GRAVITY IS WEAKER AND THE CHANGE IN THE WATER LEVEL IS SO SMALL WE CAN'T SEE IT.

MAGNETISM

Magnetism – or magnetic force – is a force that acts between two magnets or between magnets and magnetic materials. Magnetism can either attract (pull towards) or repel (push away). Very few materials are magnetic. The most common magnetic materials are the metals iron and steel. Steel is a mixture of iron and other substances.

Magnetic attraction holds these steel nails onto the magnet.

A magnetic strip just inside the fridge door holds it shut. Magnetic force can pull through paper, so fridge magnets are useful for holding notes in place.

FORCE FIELDS

The magnetic field of a magnet is the area around the magnet where its magnetic force can be felt. It's impossible to see a magnetic field, but if you sprinkle **iron filings** on a piece of paper and place a magnet on top, you can see the effect of the magnetic field on the iron filings. The filings line themselves up with the **lines of force** in the magnetic field.

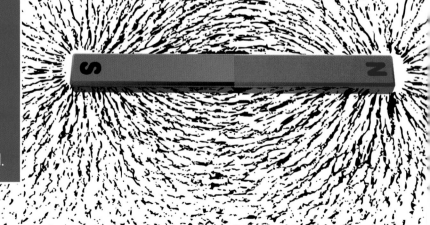

NORTH AND SOUTH POLES

A magnet floating on water or hung from a piece of string will always point in a north-south direction. A magnet is said to have a north-seeking **pole** and a south-seeking pole. The iron filings in the picture on page 14 are grouped together around the poles because the magnetic force is strongest at the poles of a magnet.

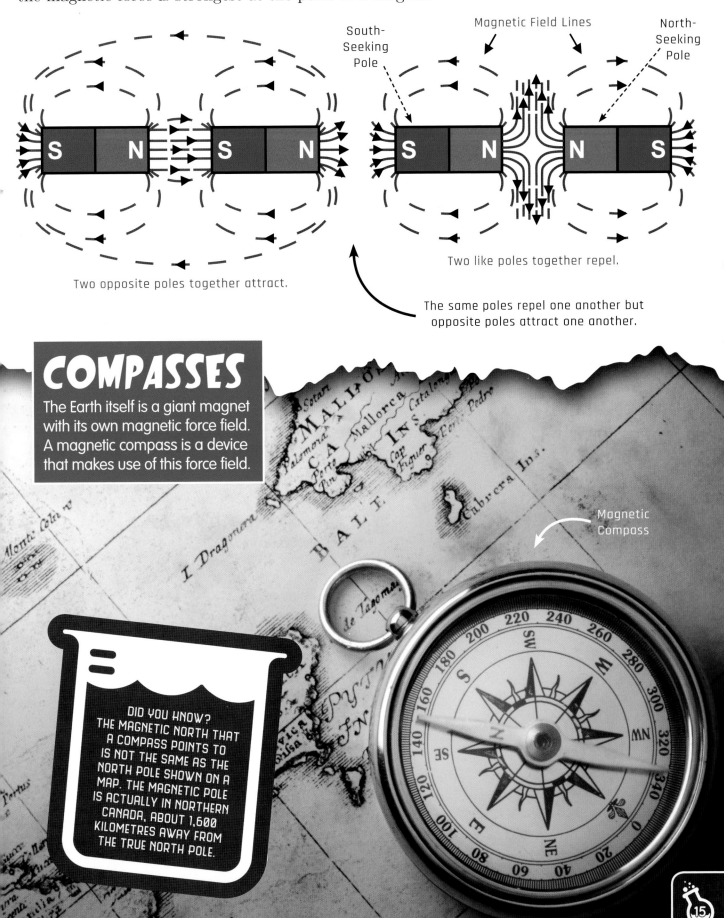

South-Seeking Pole

Magnetic Field Lines

North-Seeking Pole

Two opposite poles together attract.

Two like poles together repel.

The same poles repel one another but opposite poles attract one another.

COMPASSES

The Earth itself is a giant magnet with its own magnetic force field. A magnetic compass is a device that makes use of this force field.

Magnetic Compass

DID YOU KNOW?
THE MAGNETIC NORTH THAT A COMPASS POINTS TO IS NOT THE SAME AS THE NORTH POLE SHOWN ON A MAP. THE MAGNETIC POLE IS ACTUALLY IN NORTHERN CANADA, ABOUT 1,600 KILOMETRES AWAY FROM THE TRUE NORTH POLE.

AIR AND WATER RESISTANCE

Whenever something moves, it usually has to pass through air or water (unless it is in a vacuum). The **molecules** in air and water slow down objects moving through them because they create a type of friction called resistance. Another word for this resistance is **drag**. If you have ever tried walking against a strong wind or running through water, you will have felt it.

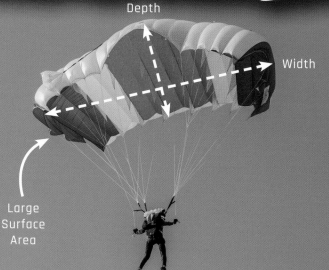

Depth

Width

Large Surface Area

PARACHUTES

Parachutists use air resistance to slow down their fall from an aeroplane. Air resistance pushes on the large surface area of the open parachute. This upward force acts against the force of gravity that is pulling the parachute down to the Earth. It slows the parachute down and allows the parachutist to land safely. Feathers, and the seeds of some plants such as dandelions, float in the air for the same reason.

Air molecules can squash together to allow room for a moving object to pass through. Water molecules, however, cannot do this, so water gives greater resistance to moving objects.

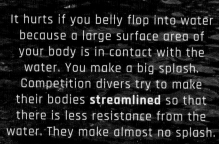

It hurts if you belly flop into water because a large surface area of your body is in contact with the water. You make a big splash. Competition divers try to make their bodies **streamlined** so that there is less resistance from the water. They make almost no splash.

In the natural world, many creatures benefit from a **streamlined** shape.

The grey reef shark's smooth, sleek body helps it to move easily through the water.

Designers of cars have to think about the force of resistance. They use a piece of equipment called a wind tunnel to help them. Inside the tunnel, a mixture of air and smoke is blown over the car, using powerful fans. Designers use smoke to see the shape of the airflow. Computers are increasingly being used to generate an image of the airflow. Wind tunnel tests show where a design can be improved to reduce air resistance. If air resistance is reduced, the vehicle can travel faster and will use less fuel.

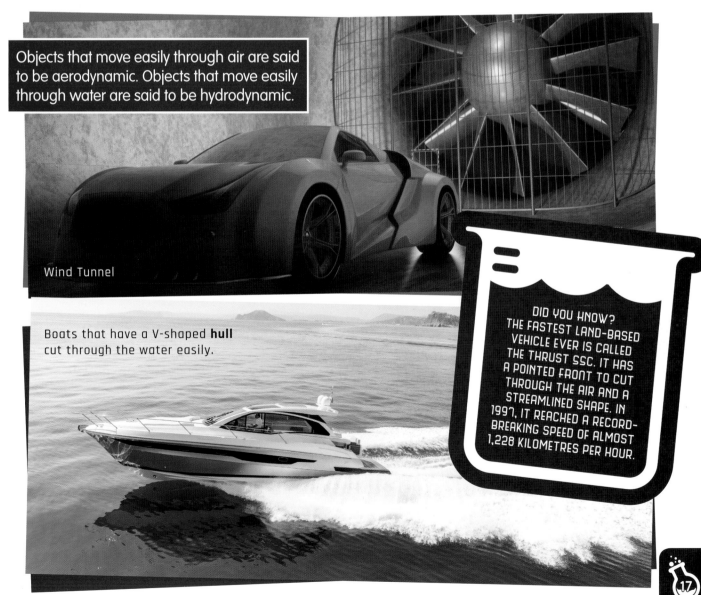

Objects that move easily through air are said to be aerodynamic. Objects that move easily through water are said to be hydrodynamic.

Wind Tunnel

Boats that have a V-shaped **hull** cut through the water easily.

DID YOU KNOW? THE FASTEST LAND-BASED VEHICLE EVER IS CALLED THE THRUST SSC. IT HAS A POINTED FRONT TO CUT THROUGH THE AIR AND A STREAMLINED SHAPE. IN 1997, IT REACHED A RECORD-BREAKING SPEED OF ALMOST 1,228 KILOMETRES PER HOUR.

PRESSURE

Pressure is the pushing force that one object exerts on another. We see and feel pressure all around us every day. At mealtimes, we put pressure on a knife to cut through our food. As we eat, pressure from our teeth cuts and grinds our food.

Pressure is measured in pascals (Pa). Pascals are named after the French scientist Blaise Pascal (1623-1662), who made important discoveries about pressure.

Pressure measures how spread out or how **concentrated** the pushing force is in a particular area. If you try to push the end of your finger into an apple, for example, you won't break the skin. But if you push the tip of your nail into the apple, the skin breaks easily. The force you use is the same but the edge of your nail concentrates the force into a smaller area. This gives greater pressure.

Snowshoes spread a person's weight over a larger area than an ordinary shoe. The pressure exerted by the snowshoe is less and the walker doesn't sink into the snow. But look at what is happening to the poles. They have a small, pointed end. When they are pushed into the snow, they exert more pressure and sink into the snow.

Air Bag

Air bags fill with air when a car is involved in an accident. They reduce injuries by spreading the force of the accident over a large area.

AIR AND WATER PRESSURE

It's not just solids that exert pressure. Liquids and gases do too. The air around us exerts pressure on everything, including us. If our bodies didn't push back with equal pressure, we would be crushed! If you swim under water, the pressure of the water increases the deeper you go because the weight of the water around you increases.

When food is shrink wrapped, air is sucked out to keep the food fresh. The pressure of the air outside presses the plastic flat against the food. The food exerts an equal force against the plastic.

Liquids and gases change their shape, depending on the container they are in. They exert pressure outwards in all directions.

The milk exerts pressure against the sides and bottom of the jug and glass.

ATMOSPHERIC PRESSURE

Atmospheric pressure is the force of the air that is pressing down on the surface of the Earth.
It is measured in millibars (mb). Changes in atmospheric pressure affect our weather.
Low pressure brings bad weather.
High pressure brings sunny, settled weather.
A barometer is a piece of equipment used to measure atmospheric pressure.

Look at the figures on the inside circle. They show pressure in millibars. During a hurricane, the needle swings round to about 910 mb.

Barometer

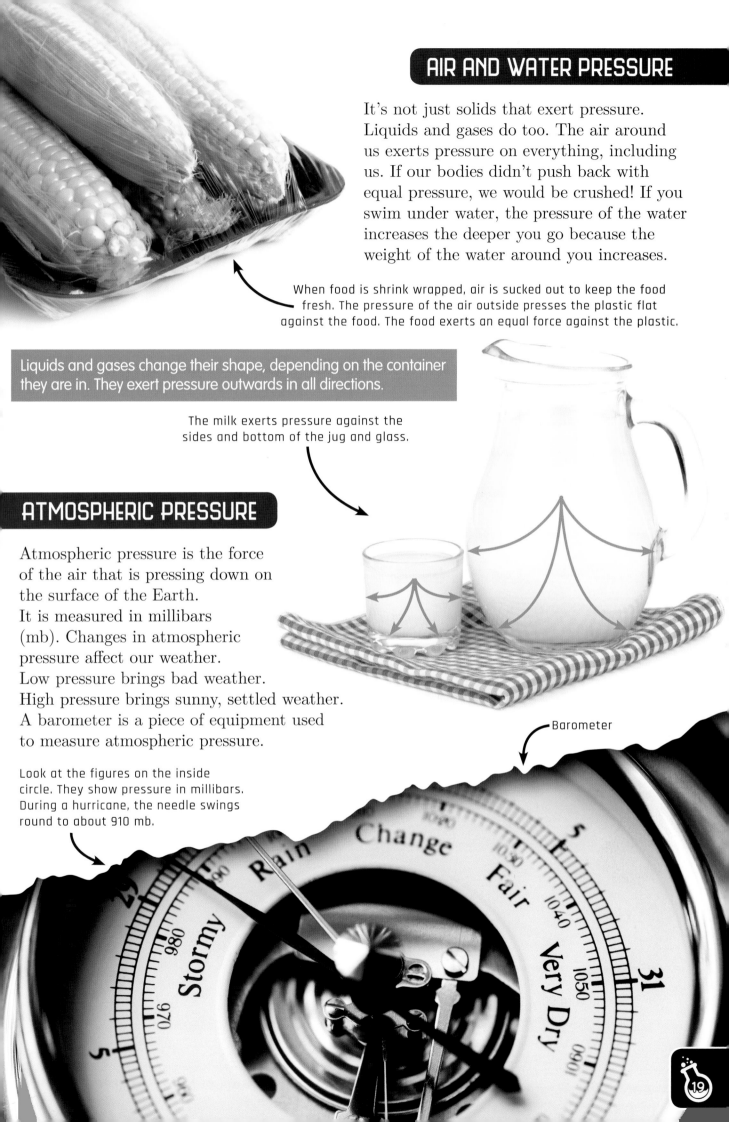

BALANCED FORCES

We say that two forces are balanced when the size of a force acting in one direction is matched by the size of a force acting in the opposite direction. Imagine you are trying to push something heavy that won't move, such as a car. Your pushing force has to overcome the force of the static friction that is holding the car in place. If the car still won't move it's because the forces are balanced. Balanced forces are also at work if an object keeps moving in one direction without speeding up or slowing down.

The arrows are the same size because equal force is acting in both directions.

In a tug-of-war, if the rope is not moving, it means that the pulling forces in each direction are balanced.

BUOYANCY

A buoyant object is an object that can float. When something is placed in water, it pushes away – or displaces – some of the water.

The displaced water pushes back on the object with a force called **upthrust**. If the force of the upthrust equals or is greater than the downward force of the weight of the object, such as a boat, the object floats. The forces are balanced. The weight of the object and the weight of the water it displaces are equal. Container ships have to be carefully loaded to make sure that they stay afloat. If a ship is overloaded and its weight is greater than the upthrust of the water it displaces, it will sink.

The ancient Greek, Archimedes (287-212 BC), was the first person to explain displacement. He noticed that when he stepped into and out of his bath, the water level rose and fell.

The ship's large surface area spreads out the weight of the ship and its containers, which means **upthrust** keeps the ship afloat.

UNBALANCED FORCES

SINK OR SWIM?

So why does a rubber ball float while a rock of the same size sinks? **Density** measures the amount of matter in an object compared to its **volume**. Rock has a greater density than rubber because its particles are more tightly packed together.

An object will only float if its density is the same or less than the density of the water. If an object has greater density than the water, its weight is not balanced by the upthrust of the water. The forces are unbalanced and it sinks.

Who is going to win this arm wrestling competition? In the picture, both boys are pushing equally and the forces are balanced. But if one boy pushes harder than the other, the forces will become unbalanced and he will push his friend's hand down to the floor.

FLIGHT

Birds are able to fly because of the curved shape of their wings. This shape is called an aerofoil. As this curved shape moves through the air, it splits the flow of air coming towards it. Some travels over the top of the wing and some travels underneath. The air going over the curved top has further to travel and its pressure falls. The air going underneath has a higher pressure and pushes upwards on the wings. The unbalanced pressures produce an upwards force called lift.

The curved shape of this gull's wings help it to fly by creating lift.

The wings of aeroplanes and gliders and the blades of helicopters use a similar design to that of a bird's wing. Gravity tries to pull everything down to the ground. In order to fly, an object must have enough lift to overcome gravity.

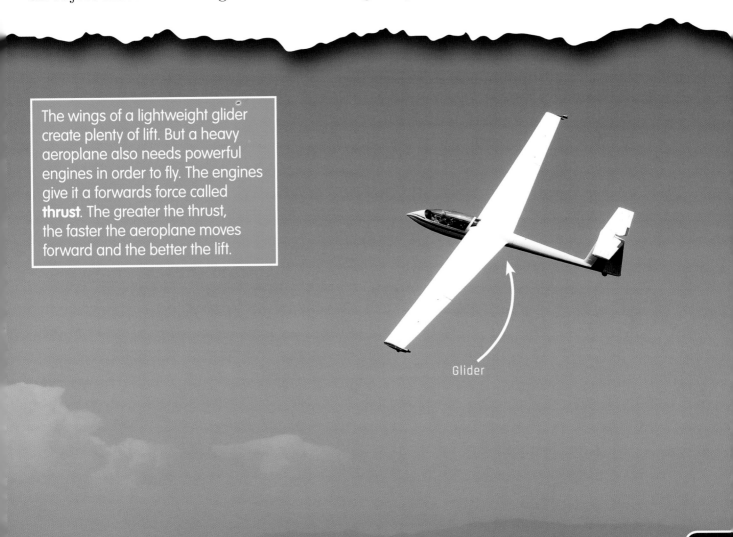

The wings of a lightweight glider create plenty of lift. But a heavy aeroplane also needs powerful engines in order to fly. The engines give it a forwards force called **thrust**. The greater the thrust, the faster the aeroplane moves forward and the better the lift.

Glider

MAKING FORCES BIGGER

Magnifying something means making it bigger. Machines help us to do work by magnifying a force. You use simple machines such as scissors, wheels or a can opener every day – probably without even realising that they are machines.

LEVERS

A lever is a rod that pivots – or turns – at a fixed point, called the **fulcrum**. Levers can help us to move a heavy load.

A seesaw is a type of simple lever. You probably wouldn't be able to lift a friend if you were standing next to them. But if they sit on the end of a seesaw, you can lift them easily by pressing on the other end. You need a lever to open a tin of paint. You can make a lever by hooking a metal rod or a screwdriver under the lid. As you press on the other end, you magnify the small amount of downwards force from your hand into a strong upwards force that pushes off the lid.

Pliers

Fulcrum

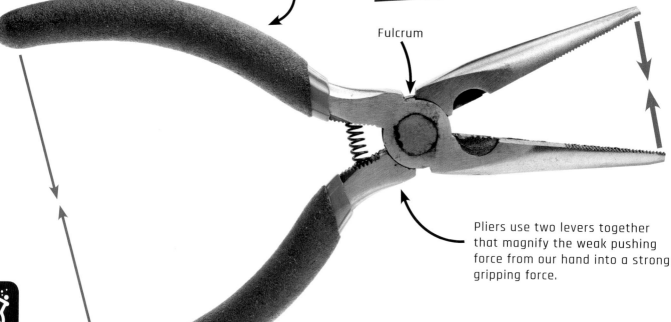

Pliers use two levers together that magnify the weak pushing force from our hand into a strong gripping force.

GEARS

Gears are wheels or cogs that have teeth around their edges. The teeth fit into one another so that turning one gear makes another one turn too. If the first gear is larger than the second one, the second gear turns more quickly but with less force. If the second gear is bigger than the first one, it turns less quickly but with more force.

Gears are used to change speed in many machines from clocks to bicycles. Inside a clock there are many different sized cogs that fit together to move the hour, minute and second hands at different speeds. When you're riding up a hill on your bicycle, gravity is trying to pull you backwards. It's hard work! Gears can help. By choosing the right one, you can pedal with very little force – but you have to make the pedals go round faster.

Bicycle Gears

ELASTIC AND SPRINGS

TENSION

Elastic materials can stretch and then return to their normal size and shape when the force stretching them is released. They spring back into shape because of a strain force called **tension**. In 1676, the English scientist, Robert Hooke, worked out that the amount by which a spring stretches is directly related to the force stretching it. For example, twice the force equals twice the stretch.

The bed of a trampoline is made of a stretchy, elastic material. Bouncing stretches the material, creating tension. Tension pushes you back up into the air. The harder you bounce, the more tension you produce and the higher you go.

Trampoline Bed

Creating tension in elastic materials can be very useful. A stretched elastic band can hold a ponytail in place or a bundle of papers together.

For centuries, bows and arrows were used for hunting and fighting. Bows can be made from any type of material which has elastic properties. Pulling back the bow string creates tension in the bow. When the archer lets go of the arrow, the tension is released. It provides the force needed to fire the arrow.

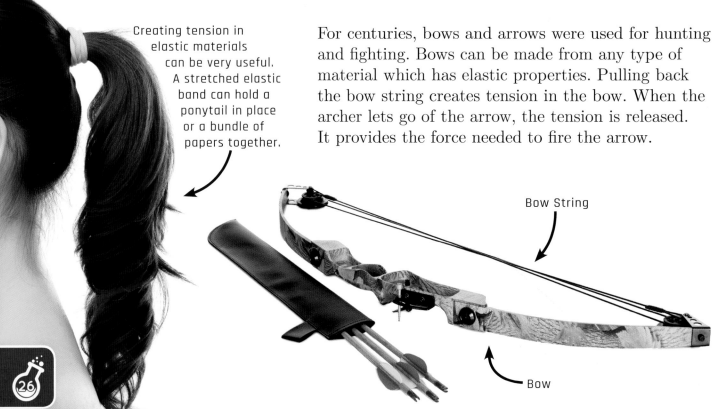

Bow String

Bow

SPRINGS

A spring is a wire that has been made into the shape of a coil. Open-coil springs have spaces between the coils, so that the coils can be squashed together. The force needed to squash the spring creates a strain force called **compression** in the coils.

The jack-in-the-box sits on an open-coil spring. Putting the lid on the box squashes the spring and creates compression force in it. When the lid is lifted, compression force makes the spring go back to its original shape and length. The clown springs back up.

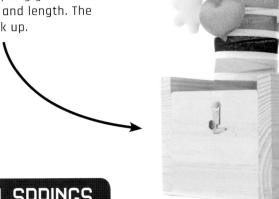

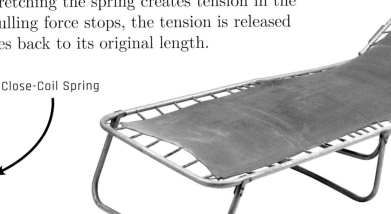

Open-Coil Spring

CLOSE-COIL SPRINGS

Close-coil springs have no gaps between the coils, so they can only be pulled and stretched. They cannot be squashed or compressed. Stretching the spring creates tension in the coils. When the pulling force stops, the tension is released and the spring goes back to its original length.

Close-Coil Spring

Close-coil springs are found on camp beds and trampolines.

SPIRAL SPRINGS

Spiral springs are often found in wind-up toys. Turning the key winds a metal strip inside the toy into a spiral-shaped spring. When you stop turning the key, the tension in the spring is released to push the toy forwards.

FORCES IN SPORT

Do you have a favourite sport that you like to take part in or watch? Let's think about some of the forces that might be involved.

FOOTBALL

When the ball is still, static friction stops it moving. If you put your boot on top of the ball, the downwards pushing force of your foot and the upwards pushing force of the ground may change the shape of the ball by squashing it. When you kick the ball, you exert a pushing force that makes it move through the air. Air resistance slows the ball down. If the goalkeeper catches the ball, the pushing force of his or her hands makes the ball stop. When the goalkeeper dives for the ball, gravity pulls them to the ground. If you score, the net stretches, creating tension.

Several different forces act on a sailing boat at the same time. Gravity pulls the boat downwards. Upthrust pushes it upwards. Water resistance slows the boat down. Wind fills the sails and pushes the boat forwards. All these different forces added together are called the resultant force.

DRAGSTER RACING

Dragsters are racing cars that cover a short distance in a straight line. They accelerate very quickly and the driver feels g-force. A dragster has a streamlined shape to reduce air resistance. This helps it to reach its maximum speed very quickly. The spoiler on the back works like the opposite of an aeroplane wing. Instead of creating lift, it creates downwards force that gives better grip. This force is called downforce. At the end of the race, the driver hits a switch to make a parachute come out of the back of the dragster. The parachute gives air resistance that slows the dragster down quickly.

EXPERIMENTS WITH FORCES

Try opening a tightly closed jar. Difficult, isn't it? Now put on a pair of rubber gloves and try again. You should notice that it's much easier. The gloves increase friction between your hands and the lid. Now cover your hands in washing up liquid and try again with another jar. What do you notice? The liquid acts as a lubricant, making it harder for you to grip the lid.

Have you ever seen the trick where someone proves they can lie on a bed of nails? Surely it should hurt – but it doesn't! You can see how this trick works using two large ripe tomatoes and some drawing pins. If you rest a tomato on one pin, the skin breaks. Now balance the other tomato on lots of pins. The skin doesn't break. The pressure is reduced because the pushing force of the tomato is spread out over all the pins.

Ask an adult to help you make some holes in the side of an empty plastic bottle. Make one near the top, one in the middle and one near the bottom. Now fill the bottle with water and watch the water spray out. Which hole sprays the water the farthest? The deeper the water is, the greater the pressure, so the water should travel farthest out of the bottom hole.

GLOSSARY

attract   pull or draw towards

B.C.   meaning 'before Christ', it is used to mark dates that occurred before the starting year of most calendars

bearings   balls placed between two moving surfaces that reduce the amount of contact between the surfaces and so reduce friction

compression   the strain force created when a spring is squashed

concentrated   increased in strength or proportion

density   the mass of a substance compared to its volume

drag   the force of friction that slows down an object moving through air or water

exerts   applies a force, influence or quality

fulcrum   the point on which a lever rests, where it turns or pivots

gravity   the force that attracts physical bodies together and increases in strength as a body's mass increases

grip   the ability of something, such as a tyre or shoe, to have firm contact with the ground

hull   the main body of a ship or boat, including the bottom, sides and deck

iron filings   tiny pieces of iron that move easily in a magnetic force field

lines of force   lines which show the strength and direction of the magnetic force around a magnet

matter   substances from which things are made

molecules   particles made up of two or more of the very tiniest particles, called atoms, tightly bonded together

newtons   basic units of force

orbits   travels in a continual, curved path around another planet, star or moon

philosopher   a person who studies the nature of knowledge, reality and existence

physical   relating to a body

pole   the point at either end of a magnet where its magnetic field is strongest

repel   to push away

streamlined   designed with a form that presents very little resistance to air or water

tension   the strain force created when a spring is stretched

theory   an idea used to explain something

thrust   the force that moves an aeroplane or rocket forwards

upthrust   the upwards pushing force that a liquid (or gas) exerts on something floating in it

volume   the amount of space that something takes up

INDEX